Arrivals and Departures

Poems

Philip Ramp

Fomite
Burlington VT

Copyright © 2021 Philip Ramp
All rights reserved. No part of this book may be reproduced in any form or by any means without the prior written consent of the publisher, except in the case of brief quotations used in reviews and certain other noncommercial uses permitted by copyright law.

ISBN-978-1-953236-41-8
Library of Congress Control Number: 2021942444

Fomite
58 Peru Street
Burlington, VT 05401
www.fomitepress.com
8/16/2021

To Sarah as always

Contents

Dick in Greece	1
Elusive Return	4
Survivor	7
On Healing the Night	12
Renovations	15
Dope and Ice-Cream	16
An Evening in the Embrace of America	20
Role	25
Night Bus	29
Glare Ice and Out of Gas	32
Mr. Billy	35
Self-Abuse	38
Flea Market	39
Nickels	42
Inside the Crystal Ball	44
Fourth of July Miscellany	46
Slick Violence	49
Computers	52
Old Friends	55
Threshold	58
That's Incredible	59
The Twisted Child of God	61
Loss of Memory	64
Southern California, Early Morning	67
Mr. Steak	70
Another Departure Reached	73
Childhood Home	76
On the Present and Old Friends Who Live in It as if It Were the Past	79
And Yet the Ground Glow Stayed Dead Even	84
Picnic	86
Leaving	88
Dick Is Gone	90

Dick in Greece

Motorbikes probed the streets like wasps a mound of grapes
smoke expanded, a boneless genie
smearing the evening muscatel
caressing the buildings, insinuating itself like a lover
deep into the green tissues of the town.
When the island is sufficiently bewitched
it will be smothered.
But to hell with another chunk of the future,
we had our magic too
the taverna's doors flung wide, expansive as a god's thirst.

She limped toward us from the back, invisible shovel
in hand, digging, digging — which was as
it should be, being the poet she is.
Her whisper, set on loud, circled the room, others turned,
glanced, really whispered: "come out", she said…
"you have to see…you won't believe…help me…"

It was late enough to be dark but not dark enough to be late.
People ignored the whole business
in this minimal Eden of one fruitless tree,
leaned toward each other in this pretend… consanguinity
disguising themselves in night chuckles so as not to be seen doing it.

The poet opened a trench to her table —
a playwright there hunched in paunch, obscured in fat
his nimble monologues now ended, leaving
him to swell silently in the inescapable scenario of his life
hope long drained in two rivulets from his eyes.

No matter, this wasn't what we wouldn't believe.
It was Dick. Dick flinging out notions

like a crazed housewife at a clearance sale, building his
own heap of factory seconds,
Dick growling, jerking, diving back for more
while his woman nodded stiffly, blinked like a doll
couldn't count on her for anything
except to make six of us, a bullshit quorum, that is.

Early Dick:
I'm telling you: women took over the world in 1968.
I'm telling you: our leaders are dressed in drag.
I'm telling you: Gus Hall and Angela Davis weren't a drag.
I'm telling you: The Soviet Union was nobody's transvestite!

I was wrong, his woman wasn't stiff, she was so loose
she'd lost her neck.
Her eyes slid toward each other like secret
lovers, then slid back as they caught a glimpse
of gleaming glass, slid yet again as
the gleam eluded her, her face
stretching until it became a soft, shapeless moan.
Had someone slipped under the table?
No, only her hands were out of sight.
She looked down, found them, simpered.

The poet dug like a demon from her chair but Dick
wasn't about to fall into any pit —
one he didn't dig himself anyway. I got up with a vague idea
of giving him a friendly sudden shove,
stumbled, somehow wound up in my glass.
My wife seemed stunned though
smiling: it couldn't be eternal so it wasn't Hell.
The playwright belched.

Middle Dick:

I'm telling you: real believers cut off their balls.
I'm telling you: Hitler was nuts but his God didn't have any.
I'm telling you: Marx and baseball can take care of this.
I'm telling you: my dreams are rock hard but can still dangle!

Now an English couple in a "delicate condition"
damn near derailed old Dick because...
because she'd sampled damn near every fertility
spring in Greece
but wouldn't let on which one had the semen.
The guy blew it. He'd dated Maggie
Thatcher but couldn't even remember the shape of her
tits just that she liked to keep them
together. Dick howled with understanding while his
broad gurgled from the depths of it.

Late Dick:
I'm telling you: I'm tri-lingual, do three times three poems every day.
I'm telling you: an invasion is a poem in any language.
I'm telling you: I'll be a line yet in the communist epic.
I'm telling you: poets pain in light!

Oh, but the doors seemed so much wider when we emerged
more than they'd ever been before.
By then the evening had beached in the sky's cave —
borrowed from the sea that found it too large
to use — night's black and glinting dome
seemed tongue-tied by such magnificence but Dick always had
his hanging loose and he reared back and told it
he'd prove it wrong some day.
"Look the stars are all exclamations!"
and pointed at himself as if he alone knew what they were so excited about!

Elusive Return

Elusive morning of return.
My shadow missed the jet from Prague.
Fair enough. It still had beer while I had
these puffs of light
tumbling out of touch yet touching me.
Seems profane to call this state *lag*
when it was the sweetest of absences
soothing my perennially brooding shade.

So be it. Friends woke to all of what they were
and what I so seldom let them be,
breakfast extending like a bow slinging arrow
after arrow of this special light
carrying our most urgent messages
though, of all we said, I remember only "Well!"
Being elusive this way will always be just fine with me.

The bubble of my life awaited and I entered it,
exited, no entered out;
how easily the streets accept a bubble!
Things turned out to be singular
and could be greeted one by one
while Central Park was so thickly swathed in green
and tree and air it seemed like
an abstract of all that nature could ever want to be.

I may have been alone in this attitude toward the day
for an office worker kept worrying his tie,
rolled a joint and glared, as if even it had missed the point.
Joggers tucked in, listening earnestly
to their hearts slow down
and roller skaters padded as linemen weaved

through lone figures of dark indecently exposed by the sun.
Something grim, too grim for the green I traveled in.

Back out on the seared cement it was giddier
two cellos and a flute were trying
to compose the raucous streets, while a clown in
formal attire mechanically mimicked
the rigor of need, moving slowly as death
coming into a friend's eyes — and nearby three rats raced by.

Realized though I like motion but I don't like the way
time is moved to move it —
so get moving — time flies, who knows
it might still crash! But don't
forget: desperation kills tomorrow as well as it does today.

Equilibrium maintained: perhaps I *was* the only bubble in all New York!

Elusive office of no return.
Possibilities were snaked pleasantly before me
and whisked away again before
I could fully appreciate their fine-prints and oh so subtle stripes!
Promises were made that promises
would be made; but I was a bubble and could
just float away without regret.

Once outside again I knew it was nearly over: things
were shifting, bunched, no longer one by one.
I saw, remembered rather, how many exquisite lives
had been erased completely to make that soaring splendor.
I sensed their ghosts piled on the street like so
much garbage outside a cheap restaurant.
I shuddered. My shadow's flight was coming in,
the bubble was leaking and what seeped in was cold.

Leaking yes, but still able to bound, the shadow hadn't
landed yet: it was in a holding pattern I could
tell — the smoggy clouds had clearly a prophetic shape —
would soon *be* in a holding pattern then...
and anyway all I needed was enough time to slip
through the crushing afternoon;
for even I knew no bubble could survive an urban night.

I got it. The elusiveness did last long enough
to steer me through for when I passed
from the victors to the vanquished zone of my life
I turned, and there was all my trash curving our behind me
in a wide, clean wake.

Survivor

The survivor is hollering at the bottom of the stairs
and though we're on the stairs
we pretend, with real conviction, it can't
have anything to do with us
for we're on our way up, up to an old friend's loft
the stairs broad, rickety, revealing —
what the way to Paradise, if there were one — would be like.

But could Heaven be any more expansive than her loft,
would it even want to be?
Heaven nothing but an *eternal* fire escape, I thought,
while it takes true artistry to make a loft —
and speak of the devil there she is
arms spread in wings of welcome — wide as one
would expect from a miracle!

None of us has changed a bit in all these years
(the light up here is mellow as forever).
The survivor sees none of it, would have none of it,
couldn't care less, utterly focused there
below us, de-souling himself apparently, obsessed with
reliving what he lived through — a terrible
celebration in some way of the days he spent in a Death Camp,
growling to himself in a garble of Yiddish
and English, each word stressed by a tempest of
gesture, a rage too insane to be
contained by the grammar of any ordinary life.

The landlord, the painter mutters, he wants me out.
From the sound of him he wants everybody,
everything out: out, out, out!
We shut him out with a slam of a door and walk

straight into a storm of canvases;
she sold out her show and the orders keep on coming…
museums? — why by appointment only and
we're booked solid thank you — and she laughs.

Her brushes look scorched with activity though in her
creative fever she put the paint on
a little thin and it dribbled;
just kidding, it's her new style.
And yes, she does seem to have finally achieved what
she wanted, the *all*, as she sees it, and without
allowing that to take anything away
from her, the all+ as it were, as she remains as earthy
as a freshly dug potato
compassionate to idea as a hobo to rotgut
more inspired than color imagined it was made to be.
She can cook too.

The paintings are then stuffed into slots, genius doesn't
need to be particular, it's the epitome of niche…
anyway, a chunk of kitchen (the part that's heavy
on watercress and light on egg)
is dragged onto the table,
bottles aged under art supplies dug out
and damn me: that survivor is still down there,
still at it yipping now as if he's being kicked, beaten, humiliated —

we raise the volume of our talking, slip from where
we've been, what we've been doing, to wishes
and hopes, to will be, if only, and of course —
the unending gossip of change
what it's like spending all this time with oneself —
sharing a brief look of wonderment
that this relationship has not only lasted but has
grown stronger with the years.

But the survivor down there clearly has no use for gossip
and he's not going anywhere, he's
seen enough horror, more every time he was "sent" on a trip —
and he hasn't had a self he'd want to live
with for years or at all —
and goddamnit he's not going to do one thing he

doesn't want to do and he doesn't want to do one goddamn
thing, and he's not giving an inch on that...
and indeed demanding his mile...
almost screaming by then — "I'm going to get every one
of you sonsabitches out of this fire-trap building
just you wait and see!"

"Goddamn him!" the painter cries. Her family were
survivors too, she understands but still...
she can't take him anymore,
he's like acid eating into the light of our day —
how can he go on that way, he did make
it through the Holocaust, yes he lost family
lost all that was good in his life but his life:
why isn't he... what, thanking his lucky stars?
It's frustrating and she makes a hair-tearing
gesture, *something* anyway, instead of him just
standing out there raving in the halls —
why did he even bother surviving? Stupid thought:
if he'd had a choice...survival can obviously be a kind
of torture, a death camp's ironic remnant —
none of the kissing the earth blessing we hear so much about!

And as if answering my unspoken question
the survivor keens at an even higher pitch,
only this time *he* does begin to climb, stamp really

so like a soldier, up those long, heavenly stairs.
He struggles on, implacably, slow but *terribly* slow.
the impetus of the ages that cannot to be stopped.

We sit and wait for what could be a sentence for a crime
we didn't commit: he's coming to deliver it
and thinking that it is like the last march
he made from the camp, and without realizing it our
talking has become desultory, dissipating
to moving cutlery, papers, or practicing a cough.

I'm not sure how much of this survival I can take
it's as if those bastards have reduced him to the most
tormented form of consciousness human life
can take and remain human at all —
and it is human denying that is not possible for it's
clear this survivor spends his time
tormenting himself — as if it were to blame for his state.

The NO that endures, the negative that keeps one
alive when all that was meant to be
YES has long since died?
Those Nazis were even worse than I thought
they *knew* that was the way it would be —
the Final Solution wasn't to be death or not just
death but: to find yourself exterminated even if you lived!

So it seems I'll not grasp this hideous form of
survival soon if ever as here we sit,
no longer waiting, only dreading the next moment
when this should be the time
for stories, memories, recreation and re-creation,
at ebullient ease with the complexity of living well.

For it truly is a coat of many colors being thus with
friends and if later it still fits it can
even be reworked into a poem.
But for now there are no colors only stitches and seams
for this Jewish survivor has finally gotten
to us — as we knew he would. There he is hammering on the door —
we've already opened it...will he ever feel safe coming in?

On Healing the Night

The wind was cool and coaxing as a con man's patter
and nudged us just as deftly into the park;
sheer summer of darkening green so vibrant
the night would radiate its darkness.
Even the crowd gleamed in that evening's highlight.

We picked our way through the luster of that heave
and surge and were well into the concert
field before we were aware how close we had
come to the other brilliance we had come to share.

We claimed our chunk of battered turf
crowded round with food and blankets under
shelter of T.V. cameras,
while a Mayor skipped through the throng
like a foul ball from one of the neighboring games
finally fielded by some of his utility players
what flunkeys are paid to do...anyway...

    we ate, drank, acted like it was a treat to be
    clustered there on the knobby ground
    and then it was, and then, suddenly, a real treat
    as Pavarotti finally came bubbling out of
    that earth in a fountain of sound,
    a voice powerful and sublime enough
    to interpret the setting sun
    or convince you it knew what Rigoletto really meant.

Night by then, though the only radiance was from
planes overhead playing at being stars.
The sparkling chill deepened, drove people
to sleeping bags and other cover; glowing

necklaces slithered by on the neck-less dark...
the bags bucked and twisted to far-off crescendos
as if following the trails the music left...

the field as quiet as 200,000 people should
ever be, while the monoliths outside strained up
blackly and as if they were of organic
stone, a growing epitaph that is, facing us, pointing
to empty space but not about to face us down!

It got too cold even for the sublime dark.
Cold enough the scorched city seemed almost cozy.
An odd image to be sure but we were acting even
odder: dazzled, dizzy with nature at its best,
for once getting humans to behave at
their best, both better for being best together...
and it is possible: just getting them
together is hard: best by its nature *very* competitive!

And it was disparate and it did all come together
all at once — we were hungry! Ravaged by
a divine voice we now equally were ravenous for
more earthly sustenance...
A street of Greek cafes beckoned.
We got the one run by the most brothers
and they were acting so brotherly
each day must have closed to rave notices.

Our order was as giddy as we were: coffee, sundaes,
kataïfi, galaktobouriko, beer,
milk shakes and...two hard boiled eggs!
Really! We knew we'd soar forever...

but forever abruptly ended a few blocks further on —

at the event horizon of the human black hole
of ultimately collapsed lives.
The street lights glowed not with light but fever
people dumped about like trash
and like trash they were scattered randomly,
seemed to find a place that one would
swear wasn't there and yet
once occupied — there it was: and always
right in front of you.

We treaded through it as if afraid it would break,
or erupt, while pushers leapt and
whirled, shook and gyrated:
Panama Red, Panama Gold, and drunks
rose up as if resurrected
and zig-zaged along to the beat: Columbia Red,
Columbia Gold, the group of us
moving through like quickened zombies, pelted
with half words, grunts, howls,
slang of chaos that can no longer bring
itself to order, ground zero of the American dream.

Where was Pavarotti to heal this infected night?
Were his miracles only for those who still
believed in them? Maybe so, but I also knew, as we
pulled away, miracles can at time be real not
just confined to faith and the night we'd left him
in he'd by then made sure it knew it as well.

Renovations

The street's been renovated,
revealing what magnificent stuff that
slum was made of.
Now I find well-groomed trees, well-
groomed dogs, shops with discreet awnings,
such subtle merchandise!

There they dine on our make-believe,
secure and pleasant as an air-conditioned safe.
The whole block and not a soul around.

I lived there once, or so I told myself
before I went back.
But these windows have glass,
close, have perspectives then unviewed;
the doors are butlers and the people not at home.

The listless air of defeat is gone.
The languid air of victory moves you
on — and out.
It's not that I mind the change,
it's just eerie being evicted
from a part of my past,
my memories tossed down the chute
with the other rubble.

Another kind of renovating in its way
except when I look for the stuff
my slum was made of
I find only a vacant lot, no skyline at all.

Dope and Ice-Cream

The bus driver warned us against cigars,
pipes and weed, told the hoary joke
about the George Washington Bridge,
identified for us, with monotone solemnity
the most "famous landmarks
in the world", then, finally and wearily
called out "Union City" like the sum total of his life.

The Philly station, another clone of the Great Ur-
terminal, though Philly being a self-
proclaimed "nice place to live"
I'm sure they think it's a child of their dreams.

The couple thought they'd made it all on their
own as well and whisked and it actually felt
like we were being swept away or hidden from
sight, (hindsight is more worrisome
I've found than reassuring) off to more sights as proof,

hustling us even more determinedly through parks
with arty trash baskets, ending at an Irish
pub with authentic imported smells and indigenous greed
where you get 6 oz. of beer in a 2 lb. glass —
and the attentions of Celeste from County Erie.

Being America, and we Americans, we didn't
stay long though — America moves one
along on principle, land of liberty and one is
liberated before one might make a wrong choice —

zipping past chain bistros, "local" food emporiums
and folk handicrafts, where one soon, upon

hearing the word "handmade", begins to regret having hands —
the very air sticky, twitching like a last gasp frog
under the legislated shade of colonial streets
refurbished and left for dead.

Well, that's about enough culture for now, for forever!
let's go find a highway! And finding
one like a sigh after bad sex that now seemed better
and better, as we careened past scabby
ponds, splats of foliage, and hurtled
by the Sunday crowds bunched around the trees
their cars could reach and yet
would offer quick access to the highway
when it was time to go, to go, to go and keep on
going — now that's what you call *home*!

And by then we were really going, flying low
as the smog lowered sky it seemed —
buzzing by anonymous machines and
places, and the few parts of nature deemed
worth keeping, or just no mall ready
as yet to risk trying to make
something inhuman out of it...if we have to
see then let's see it fast:
a country built to be best taken in at a blur.

We finally focused at a dark house set into
the by then yellowing day —
newspapers, screens, dogs big enough to live in,
the inside even darker, dark wood,
dark rugs, dark cold ashes, but a gleaming,
nearly blinding white toilet that
flushed out the side like a dentist's sink.

Then it was time to eat so... first the fixings
for a really big salad that can
be whipped up in a sec!
then dumped expansively into a bowl
borrowed from God. Joints for appetizers
strong ones, strong enough anyway they
kneaded my brains as if they were
made of clay, but had no idea what should be made of it...

but at least the grass also made
the lettuce hilarious, and the potatoes that
squatted there in their pan
the spitting image of old German peasants...

then suddenly, somehow, the wine was lurking
evilly in my glass and the steak on my
plate still sizzling from the grille —
sounded all too much like the beast was being
slaughtered on the spot!
And the evening kept jumping out,
as if to grab me, but before it could the dogs, —
for once! — came to my rescue as they raced
about flinging slobber like brochures
while bombing and booby-trapping
the yard and acting so goofy the threat
I'd felt finally stalked off in disgust.

Now the wine sparkled proudly and the steak
made smacking sounds on
the plate as if it wanted to eat itself!
We changed laughs to fit the courses which
was a laugh of course and so we laughed even more!
Watched the dogs' lips move to our words
as we toasted the Great American Meal:

meat, potatoes, salad, ice-cream and dope.

Then in the middle of a laugh the plug
was pulled and the fun drained
away into the evening…it wasn't late but
it was time to begin tomorrow (have to get a
jump on it, can get away in one's sleep).

The suburban tomorrow, that is, that intricate form
of commuting to nearly everything —
the 9:10 to a grocery store in another county
the 12:17 to a diner with food on loan from forever
then the 2:06 to scour the neighborhood
for local kids to bring over to play.

Anyway, our day was now so totally gone it was
as if we'd never met, but no one felt
like asking if we actually had…
the ayes most definitely did not have it…
we said good night quickly,
almost guiltily. Tomorrow may have been awaiting
them in their sleep but again it
would not be listening to their dreams —
and *that* they would never be able to understand,
in this the land of the Great Dream.

An Evening in the Embrace of America

The houses squat amid the trees like blight.
For their part the trees continue their
immemorial gossip — but perhaps they already
know they're not *really* nature anymore....
after all, they weren't voted for like the designed
lake and the paved trails
but merely left behind — as a fitting symbol
to the values of their suburban wilderness?
The houses may seem dead but
they are officially homes — for people of course
but things are where they truly excel.

And not just any old things either.
These things are finicky, have to be pampered,
hate wear and tear, share the conceit
of being the best and thus deserving of
the best as well; they may have started out
with nothing, just taking up space
in a store window but they had gumption and
worked their way up to having
their own home! Makes me feel naughty
just walking *in shoes* on those rugs!

Don't get me wrong: kids are there and in the
right number too. And they catch colds
and even somehow get dirty
(who knows from whom since no one
seems to ever be around) puzzle their way
through toys, computer-subtle, designed to
make them well-rounded geniuses
untouched by human hands —
don't want to catch whatever *they're* infected with!

And when the old boy comes home full of
energy policy, they hug him like
their mother's read to them about and he
smiles, wearily, but relieved to have
that day been convinced that anthracite,
despite all the bad publicity from spiteful liberals —

will make for them a better world, one where
these kids, fully energized, can be
brought out all polished, dusted, ready to cliché
guests so wondrously — let's face it:
so *cute,* having learned how to be both
polite and precious from jolly old but stern
Aunt and Uncle Television, charming them
with cartoon idiots to model their
behavior on... and make it just... *irresistible*!

That alone worth his trips to Omaha and Kokomo
(and besides it's rumored Cleveland
may be next)...yes, he's got it taped,
as we used to say, I-Phoned and DVD'd to death,
signs that are meant to be, of course,
signs of life at its most vibrant pitch but
immobilized so it can be caught and
appreciated in the time allowed... between breaths
as it were, making moments final
and in a way memory wouldn't, or for
that matter, by now, couldn't touch.

And it's only when the ice-cream failed
he lost for a non-scripted moment his still freshly
implanted equanimity, and took a swipe
at a curtain rudely and sighed —

missing it. But he still tip-toed to the toilet
and kept a molecule or two between
his ass and the sofa, plastic-wed.

That should have been enough embrace for any
evening, even one over as it began —
but as dear old Yogi said: it's ain't over
till it's over that is, Yogi, when it's not over
before it begins…so… I should have known
but it had been a while…anyway:
there had to be neighbors too, what's a suburb
for if not to choose one's neighbors —
and the fact they all live in identical compounds,
there's not much choosing involved —
and not much is just perfect for the setting too!.

She was sharp-edged. He rubbery. A bureaucrat
pair. She submits the papers.
He fills out the forms. So it was clear
from the start (though no start needed here –
suburbs slash right through
medias res to the chase) they give their things a stricter upbringing.

For they'd had some trouble with their
lawn on Karpathos — so being fully modern
Greeks, born in the USA and laughing when
saying "no can speak mother tongue" though
they're too fluent for me to fall for that…anyway —

what else: they put in Astro turf as there
Greek grass was a joke and then they made one about
"grass" and *grass* and so on. And when
their yacht got zilch to the gallon
they took revenge, had it painted and moored

("made it feel like a prisoner"
she said with a good captive laugh)...
and hired helicopters to unspoiled coves.
Greece had been great: when it goes faster
they'll give it another turn.

But right then he wanted a Ferrari — something-
slash-something model and got
indignant when our host asked where he'd
drive it. You don't live in your house
why should I drive my car?
They're higher up, I saw then, on the unaesthetic
anesthetic scale and even have
a decorator in to design their non-living space.

By then I was absolutely convinced
they're right when they say she's a
perfectionist — he, supplying what every
perfectionist must have to be perfect —
the appreciation of someone who knows nothing
of perfection and thus can be enjoyed while being *depreciated*.

For only she could have put a bay window to
face the artificial lake that can't
be seen — thought-that-counts epitome,
only she could have taught that other neighbor,
(whom our hosts have obviously never seen)
how to ride his mower over her contoured lawn.

It went on and on, the host sorry every so
often over the sinful lack of ice-
cream, the guests even sorrier that he would
never be owned by his own home.
The trees prattled on and for just a moment

they seemed to be all saying the
same thing but — what a relief — naturally —
soon the night would arrive and tell us
of its plans for the stars
and only then would it be time to turn
us off and lock us up — rocked asleep in the synthetically
enhanced, just to make sure it
enclosed us I'm sure, in the embrace of America.

Role

None of the three friends had changed all that much:
maturity lay like a penny
on the eyelids of the younger man.
True, one now watches for himself on
T.V.'s magic mirror, rather than
in the eyes of those who care or did then…

anyway, while another's quips though still…
quippy have clearly slower reflexes and
indeed his thinning hair and broadening beam
are far funnier but the third
one is still tracking down health
like a bounty hunter — his calves plump cantaloupes,
his smile garish as rigor (*immortis* in
his mind probably), the same as he was…

I'm trying to say…except he's now jogging
toward the past — perhaps it's good as
it's all downhill when you race that way.
I haven't changed all that much — can't wait
just as then to get out of *here* —
though it may be just the circumstances now when
it felt like a life and death matter then.

Of course, to see them quite the way I was,
one had to ignore the kids, those strangers they
sort of harbored in their glands, and soon
found were fugitives anxious to be on their own
again, but who in the meantime have
taken over their lives as if they owned them
(and beginning to wonder if they've purchased
shares in that famous bridge?)

and the wives, of course, have to be blocked out some
too, whether they're smirking, "terrible"
or worse: just there.
Different as all get out but united in
knowing their men would end up exactly as they did.

(And by then it's also clear they own that bridge
and the kids will have to wait to get
their promised share — by then they might even
think it's worth waiting for — I can almost
imagine them sitting waiting for the will to be read!
Planning on selling it as well — who among them
could possibly be interested in the "other side?")

But since it's only for one evening, and a social
one at that, I can treat the guys as if
they'd just arrived as well — straight from my memory.

And listening to them talk I slowly realize they
think I changed the most.
Not that they say it: it's just I don't recognize
the guy they knew so well back then:
Number One bad influence of all time, prophet of
Henry Miller, director of an all night party
and every night — though what I remember most is
being alone, studying, depressed, the parties
to relieve the stress though the word
wasn't in use back then... I can't complain;
it sounds, well if I do say so myself, almost heroic,
more fun than I'd ever had back then anyway.

Obviously then I've been elected for the role
they need *someone* anyway to play.

For though they now have everything they
dreamed of then, and it's a lot, in those dreams
they'd surrounded the objects.
Now the objects surround them.

They're caught in a narrowing future and crave
the once restrictive, now expansive past;
so if I'm made the owner of that past,
the bad guy, then they'll have automatically regained
the lost center of their dreams that I
as an alternative to them
then somehow... guaranteed —

both ways revitalized though they clearly made the
choice that counts, the one that *pays,* anyhow.
I'm poor, what else could they have hoped to see
in me, face to face, as it were, and be so easily
able to prove to themselves they alone were on the right way?
I don't care, for tonight it's A-OK as they
said, say... will always say!
In a few hours I'll be leaving for the rest of
my tomorrow, schedule set with pauses left
for exploring uncertainty
though so far in the trip I haven't seen a single site!

The moon has by then turned the estate ebony
and silver — it's not a mansion nor is it
a home — more like something inherited
by others who couldn't stand the
state they found it in and were not about to
fix up another's trash and so palmed it off on
whomever felt this was the best place to begin — near the top.

In any case, the stories are winding down, the wine

running out, only the garden is left
to run its course. My part of this story now updated —

and knowing I'll not be around to check
the proofs — they then turn from me, as they
should and vow to get together more
often at different times, in different spaces, combinations.

Maybe they will, they've already finalized
their time and space... but no more than *maybe*
as these tales have been stretched over
all these years and are almost to their limit now,
can't take much more thinning
and fall guys like me don't show up every day.

Well, I'm sure they'll find a way to beef
up yesterday, they have so far anyway.
Where there's a will, well, who's to say?
Even in America tomorrow has never been much of a willed way!

I say so long to each of them, and they start immediately
to dig down in their pockets for a way-it-
is-and-was clincher but I guess they left it
in those other clothes they never wear
anymore because all they say is "keep in touch" —
I'd like, really like, to say they said that without
touching but we did touch, held it — and I'm still touched!

Night Bus

The bus would be traveling throughout the night
a journey spaced with patches
of intimate oblivion, patches of voice
and gesture glaring
at the sudden Post Houses,
as they so rudely cut in my attempt at unconsciousness

the real one, not the dream-infested
one making excuses, making a scapegoat
of the past, the present stripped of
my personal myth: but distracted by the
blaring light as it turns into the semi-
dark within the bus so I can see a caved-in punk walk
by, looking like the last quarter of the moon,
wallet chained to his overalls
ten gallon hat plastered with green goop,
a shirt riding up around his chest —

reverse hand-me-down
and there's that bright-eyed woman, even shining
here in the dark, lighting perhaps
the dusk of her youth,
divided between two kids, piping up gamely
as if to distract her from that dusk.

"You know", she says, "the Shenandoah Valley *is*
God's country or as close as I'll ever
get, you know let me tell you..."
and she's whisked away by Shenandoah's progeny
who'll take a bus stop snack to God any day —

all the while another mother's list of gripes goes

on growing becoming nearly audible
but no words heard, hands curls in an empty lap...

And that's only back here in the coughing section
with the toilet sloshing like a laundromat.
The night acts neutral but given the
set, what's being played out in there, outside
there, seems as harsh, as accusing
as the passing lights
as if they know more than they should:
have they been gossiping with our shadows?

And I feel for that moment as if we
all could be the newly, the still uneasy, dead
learning that it isn't sleep and that
we'll never learn why it acts as if it is when
it's clear by now there will be
no waking from it anyway — in any way...

a death that is we've a right to fear,
life with all the chances
gone the ten-minute stops like checkpoints
in the everlasting fatigue of hell,
stops growing steadily more harshly lit,
somehow more permanent,
and the night more unbearable —

purple and searing with the light of fried bugs —
a woman always there at a gas pump
peering nowhere
a septic cookie dripping on her arm.

At one of these spots the journey simply ends
it wasn't death just a reminder

so as the bus sighs in it sounds as relieved
as we are, dawn deceiving us —
so wondrously! and once again!
why shouldn't we be willing to play time's game?

But when we're alone, six of us by now,
divining our coffee as if looking
for ways to conceal the fact we feel alone and
know we will
not be getting over it —
well, we can't help but wonder
why a whole night was needed to only get us here.

Glare Ice and Out of Gas

His maturity lies in disrepair and
he can't even pay the rent
on the shabby furnishings.
Puffy, pale, even more impassive
than is his wont, he made me feel...
well uncomfortable, hard to say what way —
as if I were sitting next to a cold dank
stove all that steamy afternoon.

While he sucked at yet another one of those
beers that have a fartish sounding name,
tossing out his woes like yesterday's empties:
attacked by an acid freak
in the Tennessee pines, he became convinced
that nature brought out the worst
in people and so he moved to town,
found a songwriter on the street,
dragged her back here
and even came to love the way she passed out.

She'd been raped by good ole' boys
and after that she tried to
kill herself with thorns, settling for a "pin
cushion" effect he said, finally heading
off for Houston
so she said, on "my last melody"
and I wondered just how far one could get on a final tune...

anyway, he went on, he still had her
little bundle of the American dream
around somewhere...and segued a little drunkenly
out of that to his new one, last gasp

issue of wealthy genes, (last drop squeezed from
that over-exploited Dream — my words
not his) genes, he said, that had borrowed too
heavily on ancestral capital
and needed constant, massive, whiskey transfusions —
liked the way he said it well enough
to write it down on a shopping receipt.

Seems they snort libido from phials
and fall through barroom windows, before and
after, crawl through days that might
as well not have any light at all.

Perhaps that explained the musty smell of years,
discarded but not thrown out,
dust on them undisturbed as if he had
some future purpose for it in mind,
but meanwhile the windows stick and the doors
bang the place so hot my wrists sweat.

A long, long silence; with him looking
at the mirror, the phone,
oddly expectant —as if he might be
waiting for a call from himself,
find out what he's
been up to all this time
and then with a sigh he finally got
down to what had really
happened, been happening in his life, may be
the reason the heat seemed to
go unnoticed by him.

You see, his father pulled a shotgun on him
and drove him out into the January

night and three miles down
the road on glare ice he ran out of gas and watched
the snow rattle against the windshield.

If he'd remembered Roethke it might have helped.
But he didn't and there he sat and
there he sits now as he did then, waiting...
waiting — for someone to come
along, but even if they do where will they
pick him up —
and will anything be open so late?

Mr. Billy

Tail end of a Southern day, the air spreading
over you like a hot fungus.
Never mind, have to see Candyland —
best sandwiches in town, which might mean
something if the town
were famous for its sandwiches.
No, they really are, just wait...O.K... O.K...

Anyway, it's late, place empty, about to close,
desolate, as if this part of the universe
were ending before the rest.
The old Greek owner shuffles about in
his dimming senses,
unconscious mockery of a Greek heroic dance.
Mr. Billy they calls him
cursing away at the black help in Greek
which they return in implacable, impeccable blasphemy —
and in a Greek that sounds better than his.

Wouldn't you know it; too late for his renowned sandwiches.
I ask him in Greek where he's from;
he glowers, looks confused, makes ancestral
sounds and brings us that coffee
that seems to flow from a national pipeline.
The curses continue, cups clink
and there are those little ripping sighs of plastic
relaxing after a hard day.
Just when it seems most unbearable, when
you begin to think the formica might start screaming
at any moment — he comes again,
hesitant, but coming,

"Where you from?" and we tell him and then
he tells us: tells us he's been in
this place 50 years, a long time we agree
and he disagrees, saying it's never long enough
that we always want more, need more,
how can once be long enough
when what comes after is even worse,
worse than being alive and alone
with your wife dead, your family dead
your friends dead and so many years gone by
it's now too far back for memory
to even bother going to have a look!

His Greek's half gone, his English never
arrived, perhaps his is a language fit for an old
man who knows there's never
been a way of saying what we want to.
But then maybe he doesn't know that,
has nothing to say that a curse
or a curt question won't cover as much
as he needs it to anyway —
all the rest of his desire and experience
going into his sandwiches, his marvelous sandwiches.

"They say you make the best." I say
"They're pretty good," he says and beams
"Yeah, they're petty good."
And with that he shuffles off knowing he can't
do better than that and better leave it at *that*.
Later I learn that was the first time
in living memory he'd been seen to smile;
its warmth and depth had
made him seem a virtuoso, if his sandwiches
were that good...well...it's clear

despite his words he has forgotten nothing really.
Nor, I hope, shall I.

Self-Abuse

The light of 2 a.m. is murky and lascivious
as a masturbation fantasy,
branches sliding across the windows
like creepy rain.
The beer cans stand between us
violated and silent;
his nose is badly burnt
from sniffing something that makes you come.
Time, accreting, makes the place
even more despicable, the air secreting
what could be the fluids of oblivion,
and even now swelling
the mucous membranes of the past.
Tomorrow's baggage already here,
and soon it too will
arrive as well — its approach can be heard —
raw and screeching as if moving up
the blackboard of night.
Memories being further defiled, repeatedly
molested, and the degenerate squirts
of his once robust imagination
will find no womb, none worthy anyway
of being able to conceive of even
a livable yesterday —
let alone one up to today.

Flea Market

The storm finished destroying God's kitchen/lab
and gypsied on down the road.
The flea market quickly took its place and
is now sprawled over the sodden hills
like something gypsies might own
but there are Cadillacs strewn around as well
so maybe I should forget about the gypsies.

Anyway, the trash department store is open for business.
And an old can of liniment is snatched
up as quickly as its placed on a stand over
a puddle, while some silly postcards
are rescued from a drip as a guy gazes at a bottle cap
as if it were the land of heart's desire
discovered in of all places: Nashville.
And *being* Nashville immediately thanks God for that!

None of it does much for me, and leaving
God out of it — please!
I was raised to see junk as junk
the last stop in the growing chaos of a thing
when you throw it away
without the services of a broker.

Don't get me wrong. I mean, maybe we
were wrong, my family that is —
the value's real enough
to the people rooting round there
looking for it, selecting heirlooms from the
infancy of high technology, building the common
past of the mass produced.

There they are, daintily stepping about in the muck
fingering old Coca Cola napkins
like they were made of the finest of lace
fleshing out the story of themselves
collecting bit by bit the childhood
they had thrown away when they
thought they'd stay new and never have
to then remember it when they weren't.
Cheap too when you figure
they tell us childhood can't be bought.

The Cadillac boys scoop it up by the yard
a dose of dreams for those who stay at
home and have a hard time sleeping.
Versatile and easy to arrange
yesterdays, better anyway than
looking back on nothing
if we must, and we must, look back.
It's yours now whether you ever had it or not,
a relief from the anonymous ache
of absence, a relief brought to one so simply
by a trinket old and battered
spitting image of what the real memory would be.

But that's not the point: it's that what
those things once took away
they now can give back with time
encapsulated in them, certain for once —
why else ruin your clothes and your
health in the cold mud?

But it's hard for someone like me to start
collecting when I was raised
to throw away; all my images are

tied to fresh-blooded moments, flooded
with day's always fresh light —
though right now that sounds a tad dull.

Well, anyway, I'll try. With this market I
pledge myself to honor today
as a past event too — as it so largely is.
Here's a book, pretty old, cover
gone and wet but just two bits and with
its title how can I miss:
Good as Gold.

Nickels

A bleak day, the air looks like depleted soil.
Boys on motorbikes circle the house
drawing a loud noose round us.

Inside nothing seems to help.
A mother strokes a daughter's back
the daughter strokes a cushion,
the cushion scratches itself on the frayed
couch that hasn't been up to scratch
in who knows how long.
And the clock's broken, the T. V.'s broken
the dolls are broken and,
come to think of it, so is the cat.
Naturally, what can we be but broke.

But there's a chance to win your fantasy
and $25,000 in nickels.
The mother says, without hesitation, she
wants a refurbished fantasy life
while I could go for $25,000 straight, any time
any way — even in nickels —
who's counting?

The daughter is more personal, less greedy.
She wants her portrait painted with
it, well, just a small part of it,
wants a little of that alchemy art's famous
for and with *some* (her stress)
of the money left over she could get
what money most certainly
can buy! Because right now all she gets
is a mirror showing flesh and orifice

what those silly boys shake their lassos at...
just goes to show: it's money that counts —
the mirror and the boys are
what you get for free.

Just how big a pile of nickels would
that be? she asks.
Well, I say, as the air turns to clay,
let's not think of it as a pile
but let's rather think of you laying them
end to end (not to put too
fine a point on it) and me behind you —
a hundred nickels or so away,
picking up what you put down so when
we met at the end
not only would we both know
just what a truly fabulous
amount of nickels it was but the way
you looked would make just
that portrait you've been dreaming of
having painted when those nickels roll in!

Inside the Crystal Ball

One of those summer days southern Indiana
oozes: a shower stall at the gateway to hell.
What had seemed corny in more
civilized weather now seemed a good idea:
the cool of an old-fashioned ice-
cream store and the one we'd seen featured on T.V.

We walked straight into the program
except the event had reverted to daily life
again. But everything in place:
the original Tiffany lamps,
the huge soda fountain of Mexican
onyx and mahogany,
even two of the show's "stars"
slurping hot fudge sundaes, of all things
and at the back the player organ
with its 180 moving parts —
but now at the massive rest you only
find in the truly complicated.

The owner came over and warmed his smile
on our praise, played the video
tape of the show
and settled in beside us
for the rest of the performance.
He's a Greek and couldn't believe we lived
in Greece, not because he's third
generation and not because
of Greece just because Americans
aren't supposed to live
where there's a lot of living going on.

Not that he said that but I'm sure I
saw it in his eyes.
Regardless, his pride soon outdid
his disbelief. Yup, he'd been to Greece
and...Yup, it was a real nice place,
his family even had some land
there yet, land...and 400 olive trees...
and a house though some old woman was
squatting on the place (how wacky
that sounded coming from him!).

He drawled through trips, people, sights
till he reached the ultimate admission
of Greekness: he thought Greek
food was the best in the world.
He sighed, tucked his longing away
got up and turned on the organ
and while the sound went up and down
and in and out like an intricate
push-up I looked around the place again.
The show had played it for
the nostalgia, but there was no real
nostalgia there: it just didn't run on the
time that brings tomorrow; it could
have all been just as easily brand
new, as natural as today, without the
natural burden of the past that makes
today such an uneasy place to be.

He came back, paused, smiled, went away
to check on the ice-cream — to make
sure it stayed "always fresh" I imagined.
No, it was even better than today.
I was inside a giant crystal ball but
not looking in, but rather this time looking out.

Fourth of July Miscellany

Nothing more slavish than a nation celebrating being free.
You're with us or else...you're not. Anything.
I've been elsewhere for a long time.
This could be anywhere. Trouble is, it's nowhere.

The stores have flags on their cash registers;
the ones that ripple in a breeze of bucks.
If this is a holiday then a holiday from what?
Beer, sure why not. But jeans and batteries?
Freedom means you get to stay open, buddy. Right, gotcha.

The woman of the house has such a big chip
on her shoulder it's stunted her growth —
she never had what we did!
Probably because it was ours.
She's smug though and swindles us rather
crudely, assuming, I guess, that with
all our advantages we must
by now be blind as well.

Trouble is she's damn near a dwarf and there
are a lot of things she needs she
can't reach on her own.
She frets and plots, stretches on the sly
she'll have a nasty fall if she keeps trying.
Her son stuffs himself with ten
rolls covered in red, white and blue goop.

Doors slam ceaselessly, people going back again
and again to where they just were,
trying to find purses, lists, reasons why
they have to shop again before they've even gone to shop.

It's a holiday...stores open only half the day...
half the night...crowds...
while you're at it get me some shampoo.

Junk of someone's lifetime spread on the lawn.
Take what you want if you
can stand to pick it up that is.
Nothing but discards, mute reminders of
unworkable days that ended up
containing nothing more than this.
Nobody wants it and yet doesn't take long
before it's snatched up and hoarded anyway,
as if stuff so tattered, so grey
just *has* to be full of hidden sun.

A ham sandwich. A can of beer. A baseball game.
I had those.
In fact two of each.
Everybody else just got a bite on the run.

Maybe it's better when your context is gone.
For if you've come to depend on
the mass-produced then you
can pick yourself up at any outlet and
there's always a clearance
sale going on somewhere; there's always
a bargain anyway — if you
don't let a brand name get in your way!

And so we used up our day. Now it was getting
to be sleep's turn to bring in tomorrow
and enough forgetfulness to
renew the hurts. The fireworks slashed

and detonated as if trying
to bring down the night —
as if practicing not to celebrate
independence but a suppressed yearning for anarchy.

Slick Violence

You have to be just as careful in your past
as in any bad section of town...
though as irony would have it
the town that called up a lot of my past
doesn't have any bad sections.

Even worse, it's gone arty, bland and
ritzy as the looms clacking
away in million dollar suburban homes.
Kind of stuff that promotes itself as
environmental crafts not souvenirs —
so much pottery, seemingly everywhere,
you'd think an opulent stone age was upon us.

But no more personal than a Burger King
with fewer places you can sit.
It's something I never really considered
before — this take-out luxury, fast
wealth, status bought from exclusive racks
collecting mail order gold and
sculpted glass ashtrays from a gallery, browsing
magazines whose pages purr.

Slick violence done to contour and content of
our lives. And I find my memories
are indeed quite blurred,
for all intents, and even more, purposes,
obliterated by the burnished light
of intense, anonymous reflections, and
from things that often prove
to be no more than holograms.

It's not the change itself so much but rather
the removal of the traces
of my ever having been there, or
anywhere and made thus uneasy I keep
moving, finding the phone book
is the only loyal thing around,
even keeps old names
the town has nothing to do with
anymore, as it seems to have been
remodeled too, like the houses, like the attitude,
(like the phones? all private
numbers now) in my absence... in any case,
I can't tell which
are copies, which the originals.

But then chains have to be made of links, don't they?
I follow myself to a patch of green
ignorance and sit under
one of the last elms left, it too ringed
with an ominous red ribbon.
I gaze at a scurrying distance bees too
greedy to bother with hives,
taking their honey on the run, racing
by it would seem endlessly, perhaps on a
treadmill, anyway! finally getting
far enough away it seems quite innocuous,
by now familiar enough to be
considered commonplace, if I lived here,
that is, never varying, to be depended on —
that is, till I remember where I just was
and how alien it felt, this sense
of the everyday, the suspiciously unvarying
that is somehow never the same —
just the kind of mood an alien would want

to create, to cover its invasion…
while extending it under the guise of technology.

If it were alien it would make sense, since it
would not only be struggling to seem…
well, a local, generically speaking, fitting in
its *personal* alien ways — something that
does not include the old world
of death's all too familiar attitude
toward us…so even the bright, bright sky that
does seem unchanged, is helpless to
relieve me of this sense of the alien…
and there must be, mustn't there, other ones
like me who left, ones who
still look slantwise at the sun for oblique help?

I find myself running through my list of errands
quicker and still quicker,
pick one, anyone, move on before I can
remember and thus *need*
to forget I ever was in this little hunk
of genetically modified nature.
The past can be a much worse section than
I thought: one can just disappear never be heard from again.

Computers

Watch your step as you will — you
can still step into poetry
and even when not in a "poetic" mood.
Today, for example, the yard is
filled with great rooted blossomers,
brightness leaping out from everywhere —
even the shadows are bright.
You've been nominated for this choiring —
though here confined to a melodic hum,
but one attuned to the rhythm,
to the *sway* of the infinite itself —
trading musical information,
as it were, on our greening moods.

I'm just about to add some further highlights
to my sketch of infinity in
the making, closing in on the poetic part
when the clock chimes —
and it's so like knuckles rapped!
Closing time for the ethereal —
I can still fly just not as high
and I'll have to have a ticket now —
so I've heard and also heard they're free
but getting the *right* to
have one does not come cheap.

After all that, the office seems so simple
not to say bland, I don't even
notice at first the thick cords slipping
off into what I imagine a den of electronic machinations.
Fingers go pittering over terminal keys
which I swear are snickering

as they assign us a definitive future,
far more complicated and perhaps not
as rewarding as In God We Trust.
You can bank on that anyway — OK, OK!

Just let me add: the good thing with a computer
is its memory — so I can be in that
future even if I'm, shall we say...*detained?*

And suddenly I'm afraid, I don't want
to go to San Diego, Sea World and the Padres.
Chargers be damned!
I don't want to be encoded
in a machine but would remain where
only dreams can hold dominion.

And understanding that I also realize
it isn't fear but rather, after
being here for even this short time
it's as if even the shadows have
lost their bright edge and in effect may not
even be shadows anymore.

But those are only *my* shadows
and may show nothing more than that
I am not of the required *competence*
to live in this world, have remained but
the whispering shadow of a savage,
one stripped of his weapons
and unable to fight his ever evolving foes
and even if he still possessed his
bloodied and mystic totems designed to
support the sky, this sky has learned how to levitate.

Have I then lost my magic or merely
left it in some unpacked things?
Has the wand passed from my world to theirs?
Who knows? But I can feel
it waving as it passes, it's of good cheer and
it's a fast learner —
and soon with one swoop
will be able to make my part
in the composition simply disappear.

Old Friends

Meeting old friends after many years
can remind us and, perhaps, too much
of what a shabby affair our past really was.
Like this guy, a doper, a wheeler-dealer then
a doper, wheeler-dealer now,
takes more, owns more now but it's
still the same stuff, sniffed and
owned in the same place.

And he's now flabby, grey, forty on
the edge of the timeless, dope and alcohol
inexorably filling the gaps once
filled by interest, and not only the one
on his loans, what he charged for rent.

Sure enough, we punctuate our fragments
with beer, hard to make them
fit otherwise — and after a few what
the fuck's so hot about a *fit* anyway!
Laugh fit to be tied at that.

And it has been a long time
so of course there really isn't much to say —
speech thrives mainly on the deceits
that weld a surface strong
enough to hold up under daily sneak
attacks so, in lieu of that, we look
at each other, then go back to the drink.

And of course, he knows the source of my
thickened features and bleary,
battered gaze as well as I know his,

knows they didn't come from
too much meditation.

Unlike him, though, I owned nothing then,
own no more now, albeit
it's a different nothing
and the place has changed.
In truth, neither of our memories seem to
be working all that well, as if
refusing to face their counterparts,
insisting they didn't have a hand
in making them, the way they are anyway.

That is, it's clear we don't want to be with
each other, here or anywhere
because we're neither what we wanted to
be nor what we were which
was based on a will-be premise that proved
wrong and neither of us like
to be reminded of our slide into a present

we once dreamed about but somewhere along
that way forgot to bring those dreams
along to keep us company...
or left in some joint like this along this way...

and, oddly enough considering what I've just
written here, we have become pretty
much now what we dreamed of being then,
only that was an image while
this is the three-dimensional reality so
our lives *have* rather faithfully copied
the essentials from those cloudy visions
of the past assigned to the past.

But who wants to admit to having such a
meager soul revealed, and one
supposedly derived from dreams as
sumptuous as ours seemed then?

So, you wake and forget, sleep and forget
 — on the way in, becoming the way
out again — smooth as a stream, surface calm
turbulence just a hidden strength
one counts on to be there...*underneath*...

and then someone blows in with your blown
hopes, ones that you've tried not
to think about because you may be
the *blower* now but have been
blown on, blown away plenty of times too —
and now, here, it's also hear
how hard it is getting enough air to blow!

Well, no wonder we wish to hell we'd never met
and that we never meet again.

Threshold

The haze smells of sea and exhaust,
further blurs and blots the already blemished
airport landscape, makes it
oddly intimate, while keeping it just out of reach —
like an irreversibly dying memory
one keeps going back to, determined to
see the beauty that must be hidden
within before it's too late
while the shabby airport just keeps things
going in and in and out making sure they're never long *here*.

There they stand, shadows really, in an open
sun-filled door, immobile amid the surge
of travelers — having already gone,
I think, about as far as they can go
and that they're only here to meet me and my
wife they've never met and after
all these years too, well it's really quite absurd!

My father straight, spectral, sucked dry
and by the years turned into a human
moon...my mother trying to somehow
get our of her face, imprisoned
with age, a smile at last finding its way
through a chink in the lines
laid down by the casual sadism of time,
clutching her bag as if it held her life.

They move forward. We move forward.
For just an instant the past is entire,
poised on the threshold.
Then we step across and embrace
what brought us, all of us, such love and desolation.

That's Incredible

People scaling hot air balloons,
people full of hot air or going up in
smoke and releasing more hot air,
dogs climbing trees, gnats
climbing fleas —
for an hour we watch the virtuosity
of man, master of the foolish:

my mother who pawned her life
to pay for my father's death
and now has to wait for his grave to
be completed, costing far more
than she ever expected,
my father still hanging on, to
the edge of the larger grave of
the sky, dreaming, perhaps the reason
he's watching this show,
of being up there — as living ash!

He feels, that is, he might still have
a ghost of a chance while
she's clearly down to the last
of her hope chest's ghosts
haunting her now like a prophecy
she didn't heed, she with her knack of
seeing into *other's* futures —
now that is incredible!I feel constricted by such thoughts,
while bewitched by the narrow, and yes —
haunting light we're framed in by
the screen, giving me an eerie
feeling that though they both know
that what they *may have* wanted

can now never be, they still
undertake to find something of value
in the dregs of their life,
and though it be the dying part of it,
at least take it more personally —
perhaps, but then maybe it's just a fear
that the light from this absurdity
we're watching is all the light there will now ever be!

And from their fear I come to
to fear that too, seeing us as
maggots just waiting for something to writhe
in, squirming ever so slightly now
in the flank of our very own nothingness,
ourselves being chewed
by something so ravenous it will
even feed on those who feed on tainted
nothingness, in fact has acquired a taste for it.

That was *That's Incredible,* so popular, so
many years ago now. And that
after all that they too got what was
coming to them, no favorites, one
and only one call!
Now, that *is* incredible!

The Twisted Child of God

From the great white fortress of the faith in Patmos
to the great white fortress of the hate
in Alabama: a journey paid for by depleting
ancestral light of any illumination it might once have had.

Face broad, set in lard, features dimming from
her inner dark, just barely Greek
enough to still sweat without needing a deodorant —
though she says it's like a nigger writing a letter.

Anyway, she's all woes not just disgustingly woeful,
woebegone but the woe is on me I think,
and — and she goes on listing those "one more"
things she'd found to hate — and these bitter
complaints fall from her lips monotonously as the
litany of one who has fallen from grace.

A stroke at forty while giving birth, leg still stricken
by the twisted seed of Adam, compromised
womb of Eve (she implies by quoting
from Genesis I believe) crippled further, she
feels, by the pagan visions of the Orthodox, and
further undermined by the slippery Episcopalians
and those methodically monotonous Methodists
who backslide for fun getting too close to what
Christ really might have said, and then turning the
other cheek and slapping not it but yours when you least expect it!

And indeed, the sins of two world *would* be weighing
her down if she hadn't found Jesus and in, of all
places, a "born again" shack — one that like
her was crippled at birth. It's a miracle!

So the Grim Reaper better cross himself before He
goes out to bring her in... they got serpents here of a
size that would make Eden blush! She's
Greek all right has a way with words even her
garbled life has not been able to take from her.

Braced somehow by her condemnations more than she
was by "touching the edge" (her words) of the
Rapture or so it seems — anyway she does leave
the damned to their own damnation for a bit, talks of
shoe sizes, Greek coins, a daughter who
pumps gas, the Greek islands in May, why backward
people never have central heating...this carrying her

backward again to her own cold, foul dark, only
now to potions, snake bites, healers, and
holy men. Just what in the hell is she doing here?
What the hell was my mother thinking of —
she may speak to the dead herself, but has
little to do them when they pretend to be living —
and not even my mother could have been
expecting what then came as the woman hitches
forward and unloads: we have to pray for her...*now*!

Her womb, it seems, her "begetting machine" as
she calls it, is on the blink and the doctors
don't have the right tools to fix it and she can't
seem to get enough of God's attention on her own...
so she was thinking (I sincerely doubt that)
that...and she stops — clearly she doesn't like the
sound of what she just said, putting the blame
on God even tangentially... or is it putting the
blame on herself the problem — that after all *is* God's work!

Whatever the case she soon sees neither of us is in
any hurry to fall to our knees so she hurries
back to her faith — even pretending to be breathless
as she races to her now wavering, unwavering devotion.

Thank God (who else?) I've got Christ she says, I mean,
a friend of hers married a Jew and she asked her
how could you give up Christ and the friend
said (maybe after an afternoon like ours)
Christ must be awfully important to you and she
had said, she says, Christ is the most important thing in my life.

She says it now again for emphasis but in her eyes panic
flashes as if she felt the twisted child of
that God kicking in her death-inseminated belly.

Loss of Memory

So: let's say it's Bob's or Ed's or, Heaven
help me, Sambo's

and you've never been to this one before
but you have it memorized from all

the others and anyway
all you want's a coffee so why should

your choice involve any more than
the place with the most parking space, and,

perhaps, whether or not to lock the car,
to the point you might even find

yourself walking through a receding door still
reaching for the handle, if you

were born in the age of handles,
stumble past (still reaching for that retreating

door) the cash register, up to the plush
plastic counter, where you slide yourself onto

the stool: "Coffee please. Black."
to a form in a uniform bright with trademark

youth already resting uneasily, oh so
uneasily on the bones she, he, are assembled

on… they bring it, you drink and wait —
and sometimes the price of bacon and eggs

changes while you do. Of course,
you might be there with someone,

or someone might already be there who
might remember you and/or you, them, as you

wait for who knows what as you've
already been served — in any case, you start

to yak about the weather, sports, cars,
how smart Uncle Ted is, then cars, houses,

things now, things future, things past,
cars certainly, can never have too many,

sports, can never have enough of them either,
the weather again certainly, it's never

not there—got to give it that —and Jesus
if you'd only known back in 1940,

1950, 1960, 1970...the future can sometimes
be the oldest and most pitiful thing to

be found in the past. But if you're alone
as usual you'll soon get tired of waiting,

tired of scanning the menu, the drapes,
the booths, not seeing *them* really,

because the eye already knows them
by heart, shows you the one they're modeled

on instead, images the blind could see,
maybe even the dead, while on your

own *you* then think about the weather,
sports, cars, things now and...and you leave

it there along with the place itself.
And sometimes in another of those coffee

shops or the same one, why argue,
it doesn't matter, point is you can't live

without coffee can you...you realize
your past is present *in* the present and

all the time and yet there's nothing been
laid down in memory for so long

the present's become a drip, drip on the counter,
wiped and wiped away: for there to be

an is there has to have been a was.
Now doesn't seem to be happening anymore.

What's being done to us, how will we live
in this nothing, nothing, nothing of Bob's tomorrow?

Southern California, Early Morning

What nature's left in Southern California
is at its best at dawn.
Sun and fog in spirals of wet radiance,
the eucalyptuses looming,
the ice plant like fur on the hill's back
and through the avocados an
endless spider city waits for
hyper-insects to come sailing into it!
I feel I could fling a stone
into this dream mist and hit a real tree.

But the streets are, in fact, a little
too quiet, really, as if under some unknown,
heavy stress, stained by brown exhaust
or night turning the color of piss.
I take a step off the asphalt
and am assailed by a percussion of dogs
that seems to have no source:
a canine sonic boom.

Suddenly the houses seem wary, on guard,
the quiet turns to hiding,
cowering even, streets shortened by
anxiety and I'm too being
targeted by whatever is lurking in the fog.
It bristles, closes in without moving.

Ah, a car! It whisks past, driven it would
appear by a coffee cup.
Then things reverse again
and the soft grey is trailing the light
of nostalgia, if you could

reach something here, then you
could clasp your past.
But you can't reach the former and the latter,
as later anyway, is largely past.

I walk on, pretend my fingers are
weaving these wispy strands
into a pattern for my life,
while watching a milk truck being charged —
fed by a cable that snakes into a basement
as if it were up to something
and it wasn't milk.
Behind that the gentle whack
of sprinklers, wet on
wet of fog, a man appears
nods with his back, disappears.

Then things are switching yet again
not coming closer but
emptying out, thinning with the thinning fog.
Silence so strong I find myself
straining to hear it
and do catch... what could it be?
A far-off T.V what else?
But then nothing's ever too early here,
always trying to get a jump
on what, jump made, always seems too late.

I strain a little more, hear a whisper
at the edge of sound, on a rush
of curses, too far away to pin down,
then straining a little more
hear something... a whimper, suppressed
moan, too diffuse to place as
it oozes out of the walls, the fog walls...

What nonsense!
Nothing is whimpering at all, it's so
silent the sun, when it does come
up, does it like thunder!
But no one around there hears
the day emerge, nothing's dedicated
to the fire of life, no one
feels the best moment upon them.
All this light wasted on lives
housed in a solid 3 am,
never early, always late.

Mr. Steak

I know I'm harping on it but...
I hate this feeling of being pre-frontaled
in every place and all the time.
Like this joint.
Nothing's out of place, because there's no
place for it to be in — in the first place!
Made to fit anywhere,
and letting you know that's what
this place, among many,
has been especially designed for:
anywhere, anytime... *you*!

The waitresses' voices sound like they're
choking, but tinny like a recording,
and the recorder somehow
stuck in their throats —
or maybe they're just in training
to be Muzak tunes, got laryngitis
from practicing so long so they might
become proficient at musical idiocy!

People: kids and old ladies all about
the same age.
Food: steak about the size of my wallet
and probably of an equal
age and taste.
Potatoes: gone sour on the cream.
Salad: exhumed, death
by unnatural causes.
Furniture: something for your butt,
something for your plate,
a cash register conveniently placed
for money's everything else.

Am I being tested?
Are the booths saying: come on,
it's obvious —
we're not real. never meant to be!
And the waitresses coughing
so mechanically are really just crying
out: For Christ sake,
give us a break, we're just machines!
Is the food fed up: don't you
know a chemical when you taste
one, out of the food groove that long!

Should know all this by now —
you been living in a cave? — how
can you be so goddamn... silly?
You wanted endgame —
well here it is and served to you
on the most anonymous plate
money can buy cheap —
and expensive at half the price!
And while we're on it why blame
us, it was your idea in the first place!

Well, maybe it is all right for
"Seniors". They get 10% off, one of
the few concessions made to them
and since it's food, then on
the off-chance they may still be alive.
The dead don't get discounts;
at least not in here, they're only discounted
drastically, though the cost of
the coffin more than makes up for it —
and even the fanciest grave

might as well have FACTORY REJECT
written on the stone
or scribbled on a plaque in the
grass flat enough not to trouble a
mower — the future as mown not moan
leave it at that…

to hell with it can't leave where I'm
not. So I'm not going to pay
at all — which is about what it's worth.
But I do — why? because
everyone here has thought of not paying
some time —
and I hate crowds.

Another Departure Reached

Time to leave a bit of myself behind again.
Some day these parts strewn
here and there are going to get
together and try, at least, to do me in.

Anyway, morning grave and grey.
Lights off. Gas off. Doors locked.
Windows too. Bags placed
just so, pockets touched and in order —
the rituals of departing, an
induced indifference
to keep us from unleashing love
which if it's love must not now be freed...

The fanaticism of the freeway is
for once a great relief.
I enter square by square the mechanical
stampede to and from
the American Dream thundering after
opulence if only to make ends meet
at the bottom of a cliff — and the
Dream does demand you go over —
though being a dream, let's you
imagine you have wings and can float!

Doesn't matter: I never paid attention to
dreams or Dreams and so I roar
along with the rest but damn sure I'm not
following them —
over the cliff of today anyway,
for even my *reality's*
defective leaving aside any errant dream —
and I'm not a handy man.

A long, slow hill leads us to the airport.
The planes whistle in
like they just saw something beautiful.
I'm pretty sure it isn't us.

We're inside and the chores are done
except for the task of tears.
My mother clutches her bag even
tighter than the day we arrived
at this very place.
It makes sense.
It's emptier now, easier to lose.

Just as she doesn't want to lose *presence*
now as our absences have been for
so long it's become nearly all absence,
presence no more than a flash
of sun on a foggy "low-cloud" day
and probably not time enough
left to wait for it to lift, the sun would
still be unfit, watery…and anyway
there's not time enough for
either the long, or the short of it,
more like the anniversary of something
that happened long ago and that's
still observed as…as there's
nothing better to do.

We say goodbye and still don't go.
Our destination's been delayed.
Then, in the uneasy contradictory way
airports seem to work,
we're back on schedule and she

dutifully leaves
wandering away in no hurry
to be anywhere and this
has become more personal than
anywhere usually is.

She looks older, smaller, more isolated
with each step,
a picture of all our lives, leaving.
She's still strong but has no
objects to test it on, prove it's still...strong.
Longing, frustration and sadness
are taking their revenge
on someone who didn't demand enough.
Not doing the right thing
for yourself is not doing the right
thing for anyone —
sounds good but like so many
"sounding goods" always hollow when listened closely to..

Still if it wasn't this, something else would
kill us. But please let me have
no more such partings, the first
and the last are hard enough to bear.
I look again. The picture of
our lives is empty, which has come
to feel like the way it should
be now. Starting to mull the how of now
departure is announced
as if saving me the wasted effort.

We ascend, the grey layers fall away,
become light, with regions of
turbulence — and these we can buckle for.

Childhood Home

Not that it was ever on my mind
as a destination, or even
something to do, but being close,
quite by chance... well why
not take a look at the house
where I was born, one of the few
objects that remained from my childhood.
Not much really, but maybe it
would be intense.

And then I was there
but for a moment didn't know what
there was — the road seemed
wrong (paved, too short)
the other houses now squatting there
seemed wrong too (newer,
too many) the driveway even more
wrong (half of it missing,
the other half too narrow, even
the compact car could barely make it through...).
Trees were missing too, and a
rusted hulk had replaced
a tire-swing that I can remember but cannot
remember anyone ever swinging in.

Inside, the house still enclosed
the same odd spaces
but it was empty and felt, somehow,
on the...*defensive*—
with nothing to defend as the house was
empty...and empty long enough to
be declared dead if anyone
cared enough to bother.

I drove away.
The miles that had once formed
what was to become the sum
of my experience as a child
told me what was wrong:
I hadn't remembered one thing of my
life I had spent 18 years of there.
Yes, there was a recognition
of a kind, but it was
like one taken from someone else's
detailed description and because it
wasn't his, got some of the details wrong —
even the emptiness I'd so often
felt while living there
wasn't as...*removed* as this, stripped of
even my youthful sense of despair.

Not that I had been expecting much,
a little feeling of a life
once lived there, a trace of nostalgia
but one I could leave fast
enough, and without a trace —
something unreal then but warm
as if familiar — something, that is,
I could have only taken away
from there...but I hadn't
taken it then so what should I
have expected so much later?
If there had been ghosts they
obviously got tired of waiting and left.

It's a little strange, though, a little
chilling to learn that nearly half

of my life must still be hanging
out somewhere inside me yet not have
a clue where that might be.

On the Present and Old Friends Who Live in It as if It Were the Past

I seem to be plagued of late
by old friends determined to go on
living in their past.
Common enough I'll admit, but not
for that less curious — for my
friends anyway who are, were,
of the curious kind!
Full of the hopes that made those days
into launching pads for dreams —
they should have used up
their fuel by now,
but they seem to be still powering
their lives though the rocket's
falling back to a rough landing —
why be euphemistic, the impetus of
failed dreams will insure
the collision is huge and will
lead to new depths when ironically
new heights are what we were always led to expect!

Work into that the dust and dimness
of the rejectementa stored out
of sight in those niches that
fill the incurious mind...
For what was dreamed of *has*
been reached, only it's shown to
be what was there
all along, so what they really were then
not what they were dreaming of
is now made into the dream;
but the past, any past, is not designed

as a receptacle for hope —
pressured thus it swells like a
weak sidewall. When it pops —
well, you're left stranded in senility.

Anyway, I agree, my friend, I said again
and again, yes, you, all
of us were fresh and green — exhilarated
with it, back then, but we were
not free, only felt *freed*
and the difference is critical —
we felt able to take on anything,
do anything as well, but soon found we
were not able to.

Or should have for apparently you
have remained committed
to the ideal while retaining the
unable part of it as well....
for if what you, all of us, wanted
was a world that had never
been, then you should rejoice in
the bounty of your days,
for this world of yours will truly never
be, as it never was.

I went elsewhere, did other than
you, perhaps didn't find *exactly* what
I was looking for, but did
find it was worth the look,
willing, and this is what I found important,
willing, no, *eager* to look back!

But you seem to have just settled into

a that's-how-it-is mentality —
so I can only believe you never...
believed that life is all vision
but in order to *see* you have to keep
looking — all the time!
You cannot just pass through 40, 50
years and cash in the light
you used to vault from childhood
into true youth. No, for now
and in barely half that time you
have apparently found yourself cleaned
out and even though you may think
it's still all there and that you've...
only misplaced the combination.

You must know by now, you simply must,
that even if you could open the past
the light in there would be wrong —
realize too late but perhaps realize
anyway, light is the one thing that can
never be locked up, not even stored;
only darkness can, indeed thrives on that.

Maybe that's what bothers you.
Anyway, there's plenty of light right
here, where you are, right now,
that is where you're not, but could be yet.
But first you must stop trying to
dream this dream, at the very least
prevent it from pulling you along
with it as it slides into the past,
for those lands are long deserted
and indeed clearly desert now.

Desert yes, but dwelling there, trying
to, insisting it's reclaimable, can
flourish again, you will find, or worse
just accept, your vision will grow
steadily more blurred by that fine,
thin mist of sadness falling from your eyes,
the form of dew that with this
desert abides, one which will thicken
with the heat and then turn
cold when overcome by the
lurking shadow of your past lives....
when this same site will produce images
of what it was like when flourishing
though being desert clearly a mirage —
and all this while right around you,
right before your eyes, the world is
blooming, waiting to be savored, left
to mature and go its way on its own,
picking is always a mistake when it comes
to the delicate graceful things
and moments of life... *but* somehow
you are refusing to do that —
not even admitting it's there or if admitting
then as part of an argument that's
it's not what you meant it to be
refusing thus to admit it can be lived in —
acting as if you were being held
prisoner — and against your will!

While the present has an open-door
policy for one and all —
will go on expanding along the horizon
of what might have been, but then
swelling up into a real one,

not the fairy tale might-have-been —
the one that still might contain your life.

And Yet the Ground Glow Stayed Dead Even

It was the house I didn't want to wake —
it sure needed a rest from the kids!
Outside the college town was quiet too —
nowhere was there any struggle
with the day that had settled in so early.
What could I, a stranger, do but wait
and learn where I'd been scribbled
in for today's game.

I idled about the toy-strewn lawn
badly barbered as a poor man's children,
lingered by a picnic table littered
with leaves and leavings
watching my cigarette turn into two.
There were the angry, jumpy squirrels
disregarding nature in the way
animals often do, (we seem to be the only
ones that have to keep
reassuring ourselves it's there!)
clumps of moss resting
on something between mud and dirt.

In a way shabby, in a way too discreet
but of a piece, if without a pattern;
from outside the windows were blinded
by light, as if reminding me
they are made for looking out, but keeping
hidden all that's within…a whole
philosophy of what a home should mean.

Here some fat cars squatting in contentment
there a kitchen fan purring in

the shrubs, and all the while a garbage
truck drawing nearer
clanging and rattling like a summer sleigh.

Not a helleva lot to run a life on
but right then it would do —
neither good nor bad, just there,
a mystery which when revealed turns
out to be what we knew all along
except how it is we make things mysterious.

Idle thoughts, not a time for even "window"
philosophy — I was where and will be for
a while and after that something
else will surround me, hoping it's not real close —
and leave it at that!

And anyway, the house was waking by then,
stretching like a cat —
and just beyond its claws I
could imagine the unknown waiting there —
ready at any moment
to burst in and fling this lair
to the winds of countless
lives that just happened to be passing by.

And for one last moment in that yard of
presence, I watched the glitter
of unique points of light playing with the
shadows themselves toying with
the leaves, the trees oblivious, sky bound....

and yet the ground glow stayed dead even as a still springboard.

Picnic

No one wants to go and no one
knows where to go — or not to go —
but damn it, we're going and even
if the where is worse than nowhere!
Well then let's go nowhere but let's go!

Cranky with our strident lack of plan
we go to the nowhere the crabbiest demands.
Nowhere must be the people's
choice: the roads are jammed.
The thick peat-like heat lies close to
the smoldering earth
and the best beaches are all fenced off
or maybe we're fenced in, anyway,
Miss Testy can't live without the best beach.

She dashes back and forth
rabidly searching for a hole
but by the time she finds one she's
so tuckered out she doesn't go
just swims in her sweat and fumes.
Why did we go if we couldn't swim? she asks.
Swimming? We never even got
our going going! Could have gotten further
staying at home! I roar to myself.

The food is good though, that last-ditch
something you're never quite reduced
to at home but know you should
always have on hand when expected fun
proves not to be fun at all...
the beer though is "that's-all-they-had" brand.

We scatter for leaks, then wait
for someone to douse the
day before it breaks into actual and not
just metaphorical flames.
I note: black folks on a picnic have a
good time, nowhere or no nowhere,
and there's more sand where there's
less grass, and silly clothes fit silly shapes.
Squad cars move through the bushes,
ogle the weary brush.

Finally, finally! the shadows grow longer
than our faces. Hurrah!
We've ruined the day! Let's split!
We drive back to the city without a hitch
acting, for all the world, like responsible adults.

Leaving

We fly out the same time we flew in.
Then it was light and now it is night.
Summer is through with
us but we are not through with it.

It's not really so neat: the flight's delayed.
An airport is an instant
that when stretched by waiting
is bleaker than winter in a lush land...
but then I've found high technology is
winter, always winter, and even
as efficient at it at controlling its
environment, knows nothing of ours
as shown by those bare branches
grabbing at the low snow sky,
tenacious and tedious as a dying imagination.

You wait and wait and wait in the
thinning instant pass through
languages to pass through them again
patches of light leading to darkness
which never lies outside the reach of light,
learning because living is learning
that Duty Free is just another brand name.

Things seemed to drop away as our circular
journey went on. Became more and
more like a return to a few
selective bones, dug up, reburied, dug up,
reburied — it's hard to give up
completely on a bone they too should
turn to dust and grass

but it seems they never do.
And worse, I can't even remember what
animals they came from or
if, in fact, they were buried by me.

Anyway, in this way station of the receding
present it's clear we failed
this year, failed to use
up enough of ourselves, failed to
look ahead instead of back,
failed to remember that you can't
live a life just because it hurts.

Here it's clear and it doesn't matter.
Here there is going and coming.
The one is up, the other down
and it only matters that you are one or
the other and come to accept
that, at least for then.
What ingenious forms entropy can take!

Dick Is Gone

It's winter now and the summer bar is
nearly empty. The motorbikes now
hiss through puddles and go out.
Dick, the poet and the playwright are gone,
the fertility guzzler has split, has
probably split in two by now and is
wondering what she wanted with another stranger.

The owner's eyes are even a deeper amber
but it's a smudged one,
rubbed against too many greasy views.
It's been night a long time,
it's the season for it after all —
but who ever gets high on any kind of fall?

For a moment I too feel I disappeared
along with summer
and that there's nothing I can do
about it — somebody else comes in then
looking for the part of himself
he'd enjoyed belonging to.
We drink and pretend we know each other.
Come to find out we actually do
and immediately discover we have
a lot in common but then 90% of any
life is shared in common with the rest —
or so I read somewhere —
makes it feel good to be back —
such a short time to be so long away!
Only the echo of her bellowing whisper persists...

About the Author

Philip Ramp (b. 1940) was born in Michigan and attended the University of Michigan. He has lived in Greece for over 50 years (50 of them with his wife who recently died). He has published 15 collections of his own poetry and an equal number of collections of Greek poets in English translation. Both his poetry and his translations from the Greek have been published in the USA, UK and Greece.

More poetry from Fomite...
Anna Blackmer — *Hexagrams*
L. Brown — *Loopholes*
Sue D. Burton — *Little Steel*
Christine Butterworth-McDermott — *Evelyn As*
David Cavanagh— *Cycling in Plato's Cave*
James Connolly — *Picking Up the Bodies*
Greg Delanty — *Loosestrife*
Mason Drukman — *Drawing on Life*
J. C. Ellefson — *Foreign Tales of Exemplum and Woe*
Anna Faktorovich — *Improvisational Arguments*
Barry Goldensohn — *Snake in the Spine, Wolf in the Heart*
Barry Goldensohn — *The Hundred Yard Dash Man*
Barry Goldensohn — *The Listener Aspires to the Condition of Music*
Barry Goldensohn — *Visitors Entrance*
R. L. Green — *When You Remember Deir Yassin*
KJ Hannah Greenberg — *Beast There—Don't That*
Gail Holst-Warhaft — *Lucky Country*
Judith Kerman — *Definitions*
Joseph Lamport — *Enlightenment*
Raymond Luczak — *A Babble of Objects*
Kate Magill — *Roadworthy Creature, Roadworthy Craft*
Tony Magistrale — *Entanglements*
Gary Mesick — *General Discharge*
Giorigio Mobili — *Sunken Boulevards*
Andreas Nolte — *Mascha: The Poems of Mascha Kaléko*
Sherry Olson — *Four-Way Stop*
Brett Ortler — *Lessons of the Dead*
David Polk — *Drinking the River*
Janice Miller Potter — *Meanwell*
Janice Miller Potter — *Thoreau's Umbrella*
Philip Ramp — *The Melancholy of a Life as the Joy of Living It Slowly Chills*
Philip Ramp — *Arrivals and Departures*
Joseph D. Reich — *A Case Study of Werewolves*
Joseph D. Reich — *Connecting the Dots to Shangrila*
Joseph D. Reich — *The Derivation of Cowboys and Indians*
Joseph D. Reich — *The Hole That Runs Through Utopia*
Joseph D. Reich — *The Housing Market*
Kenneth Rosen and Richard Wilson — *Gomorrah*
Fred Rosenblum — *Playing Chicken with an Iron Horse*
Fred Rosenblum — *Tramping Solo*
Fred Rosenblum — *Vietnumb *
David Schein — *My Murder and Other Local News*
Harold Schweizer — *Miriam's Book*
Scott T. Starbuck — *Carbonfish Blues*
Scott T. Starbuck — *Hawk on Wire*

Scott T. Starbuck — *Industrial Oz*
Seth Steinzor — *Among the Lost*
Seth Steinzor — *Once Was Lost*
Seth Steinzor — *To Join the Lost*
Susan Thomas — *In the Sadness Museum*
Susan Thomas — *Silent Acts*
Susan Thomas — *The Empty Notebook Interrogates Itself*
Sharon Webster — *Everyone Lives Here*
Tony Whedon — *The Tres Riches Heures*
Tony Whedon — *The Falkland Quartet*
Claire Zoghb — *Dispatches from Everest*

Dual Language
Vito Bonito/Alison Grimaldi Donahue — *Soffiata Via/Blown Away*
Antonello Borra/Blossom Kirschenbaum — *Alfabestiario*
Antonello Borra/Blossom Kirschenbaum — *AlphaBetaBestiaro*
Antonello Borra/Anis Memon — *Fabbrica delle idee/The Factory of Ideas*
Tina Escaja/Mark Eisner — *Caida Libre/Free Fall*
Luigi Fontanella/Giorgio Mobili — *L'Adoescenza e la note/Adolescence and Night*
Aristea Papalexandrou/Philip Ramp —*Μας προσπερνά/It's Overtaking Us*
Katerina Anghelaki-Rooke//Philip Ramp — **Losing Appetite for Existence**
Jeannette Clariond/Lawrence Schimel — *Desert Memory*
Mikis Theodoraksi/Gail Holst-Warhaft — *The House with the Scorpions*
Paolo Valesio/Todd Portnowitz — *La Mezzanotte di Spoleto/Midnight in Spoleto*

For more information or to order any of our books, visit:
http://www.fomitepress.com/our-books.html

Writing a review on Amazon, Good Reads, Shelfari, Library Thing or other social media sites for readers will help the progress of independent publishing. To submit a review, go to the book page on any of the sites and follow the links for reviews. Books from independent presses rely on reader-to-reader communications.

www.ingramcontent.com/pod-product-compliance
Lightning Source LLC
Chambersburg PA
CBHW021429070526
44577CB00001B/128